THE IRELAND
COLOURING BOOK

First published 2016

The History Press Ireland
50 City Quay
Dublin 2
Ireland
www.thehistorypress.ie

The History Press Ireland are a member of Publishing Ireland,
the Irish book publisher's association.

Text © The History Press, 2016
Illustrations by Lucy Hester © The History Press, 2016

British Library Cataloguing in Publication Data.
A catalogue record for this book is available from the British Library.

ISBN 978 1 84588 908 1

Typesetting and origination by The History Press

THE IRELAND
COLOURING BOOK

PAST AND PRESENT

St Fin Barre's Cathedral, County Cork. ▸

The Grand Opera House, Belfast. ▶

A hurling match – the Defence Forces vs BOI. ▶

Belfast City Hall. ▶

Skellig Michael. ▶

Four women selling fish on Spanish Parade on the
Spanish Arch side of the Claddagh in Galway City, *c.* 1905. ▶

Dublin Castle. ▶

Knockpatrick Gardens, near
Foynes, County Limerick. ▶

Fishermen on the pier at Downings,
County Donegal, *c.* 1910. ▸

Kinsale, County Cork. ▶

A rural scene from Westport,
County Mayo, *c*. 1900. ▶

Christ Church Cathedral, Dublin. ▸

Locomotive 107 at Valentia (Valencia)
Harbour Station in County Kerry, *c.* 1905. ▸

The Temple Bar area of Dublin. ▶

Cloondara Harbour on the
Royal Canal, County Longford. ▸

Sligo Races. ▶

St Patrick's Cathedral, Dublin. ▸

Powerscourt Estate, Dublin. ▶

SS *Nomadic* and the Titanic Belfast
Museum in the background. ▶

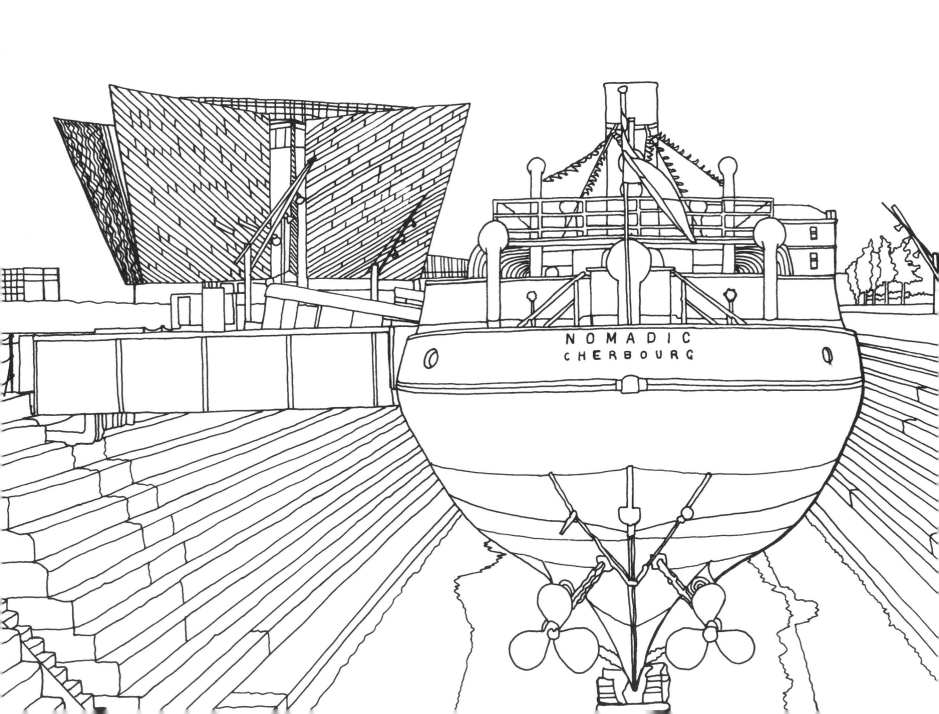

Malahide Castle, County Dublin. ▶

The Giant's Causeway. ▸

Adare, County Limerick. ▸

Galway Harbour. ▶

Locomotive yard, Ballinamore,
County Leitrim, 1959. ▸

Irish dancing. ▸

Youghal, County Cork. ▸

The river and village of Avoca, County Wicklow.

Irish travellers. ▶

Blarney Castle, County Cork. ▸

English Market, Cork. ▶

National Museum of Ireland, Dublin. ▶

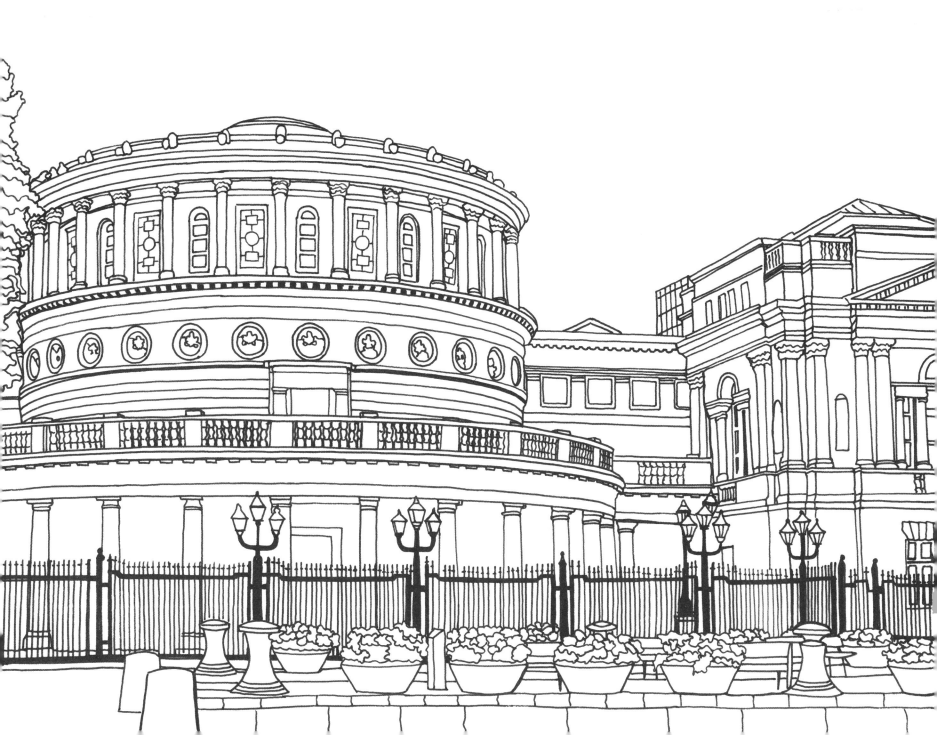

Stradbally Steam Railway, County Laois. ▶

Donkey rides at Kilkee,
County Clare, *c.*1863–1880. ▸

The weir on the Shannon at Athlone,
County Westmeath, *c.* 1895. ▸

Harvesting scene from the Lawrence
Collection Irish Life series, *c.* 1897. ▶

Cobh, County Cork. ▸

Tourists motoring past Tunnel Cottage or
Long Tunnel Cottage, Glengariff, County Cork, 1906/7. ▸

Claddagh lobster pots, County Galway. ▸

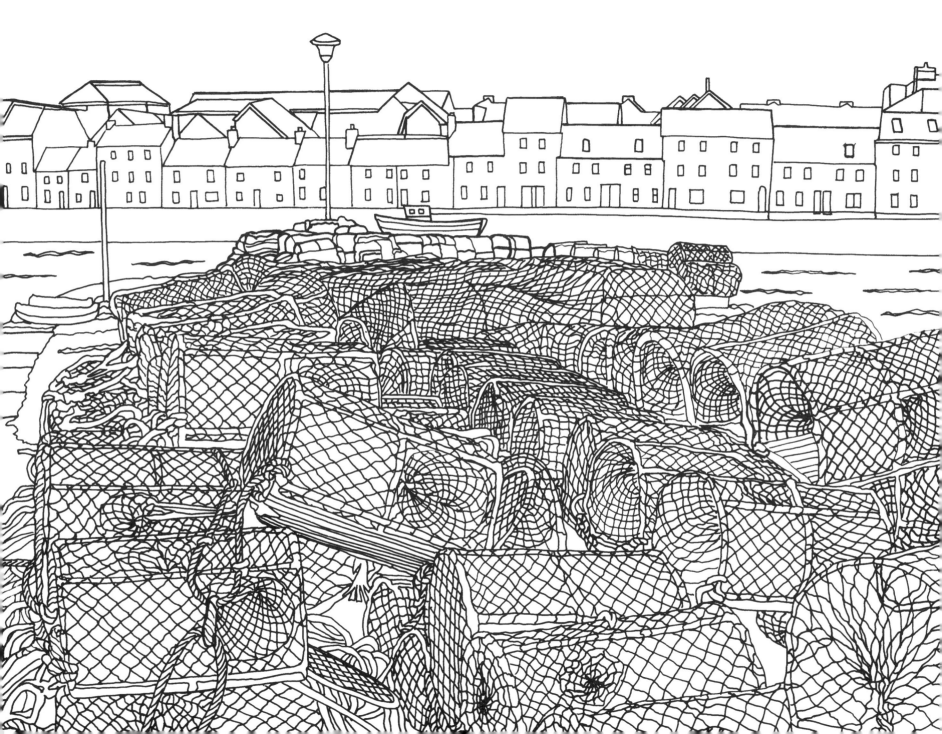

Trinity College, Dublin. ▶

Rock of Cashel, County Tipperary. ▸

The Hook Lighthouse, County Wexford. ▶

Athlone and the River Shannon. ▸

Dublin Zoo. ▶

A Gaelic football match – the Defence
Forces vs BOI at Semple Stadium. ▸

Jeanie Johnston, docked at Custom House Quay in Dublin. ▶

The illustrations in this book have been created with thanks to the following sources:

St Fin Barre's Cathedral, County Cork. (By kind permission of Saint Fin Barre's Cathedral. Based on a photograph by Todd Slagter, Flickr)

The Grand Opera House, Belfast. (Based on a photograph by Jessica Spengler, Flickr)

A hurling match – the Defence Forces vs BOI. (Based on a photograph by Irish Defence Forces, Wikimedia Commons)

Belfast City Hall. (Based on a photograph by Jennifer Boyer, Flickr)

Skellig Michael. (By kind permission of The Skellig Experience Visitor Centre. Based on a photograph by Don Richards, Flickr)

Four women selling fish on Spanish Parade on the Spanish Arch side of the Claddagh in Galway City, *c.* 1905. (Based on a photograph from the National Library of Ireland Commons Collection, Ref.: Eas 4055)

Knockpatrick Gardens, near Foynes, County Limerick. (By kind permission of Knockpatrick Gardens. Based on a photograph by IrishFireside, Flickr)

Fishermen on the pier at Downings, County Donegal, *c.* 1910. (Based on a photograph from the National Library of Ireland Commons Collection Ref.: CDB51)

Kinsale, County Cork. (Based on a photograph by Ludovic Péron, Flickr)

A rural scene from Westport, County Mayo, *c.* 1900. (Based on a photograph from the National Library of Ireland Commons Collection, Ref.: Eas 4077)

Christ Church Cathedral, Dublin. (By kind permission of Christ Church Cathedral. Based on a photograph by Psyberartist, Flickr)

Locomotive 107 at Valentia (Valencia) Harbour Station in County Kerry, *c.* 1905. (Based on a photograph by Robert French of Lawrence Photographic Studios, Dublin, National Library of Ireland Commons Collection, Ref.: L_CAB_06562)

The Temple Bar area of Dublin. (Based on a photograph by Leandro Neumann Ciuffo, Flickr)

Cloondara Harbour on the Royal Canal, County Longford. (Based on a photograph by Sarah 777, Wikimedia Commons)

Sligo Races. (Based on a photograph courtesy of Sligo Races)

St Patrick's Cathedral, Dublin (Based on a photograph by Tony Webster, Flickr)

Powerscourt Estate, Dublin. (By kind permission of Powerscourt Gardens. Based on a photograph by Wendy Cutler, Flickr)

SS *Nomadic* and the Titanic Belfast Museum in the background. (By kind permission of Titanic Belfast. Based on a photograph by Nico Kaiser, Flickr)

Malahide Castle, County Dublin. (By kind permission of Malahide Castle. Based on a photograph by Ian Hunter, Flickr)

The Giant's Causeway. (By kind permission of the National Trust. Based on a photograph by Jack Shainsky, Flickr)

Galway Harbour. (Based on a photograph by Eoin Gardiner, Flickr)

Locomotive yard, Ballinamore, County Leitrim, 1959. (Based on a photograph by James P. O'Dea from the National Library of Ireland Commons Collection, Ref.: ODEA 8/76)

Irish dancing. (Based on a photograph by Adam Baker, Flickr)

The River and village of Avoca, County Wicklow. (Based on a photograph by Sarah777, Wikimedia Commons)

Youghal, County Cork. (Based on a photograph by Meg Marks)

Also from The History Press

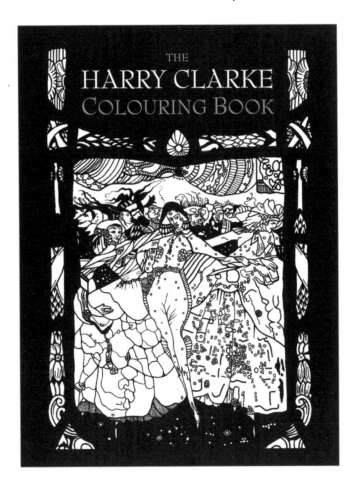